CLYDE STEAMERS
REMEMBERED

Published by the Paddle Steamer Preservation Society (Scottish Branch)
April 1994

CLYDE STEAMERS REMEMBERED

Twenty five years ago, the Scottish Branch of the Paddle Steamer Preservation Society was founded by enthusiasts determined to maintain the tradition of sailing by steamer on the beautiful Firth of Clyde. Within just a few years, that determination had paid off handsomely and *Waverley*, the last sea-going paddle steamer in the world, had been sold to the Society for £1. But that was not the end of the story: ever since *Waverley* returned triumphantly to service in 1975 she has depended for her survival on the efforts not only of her devoted Board of Directors and staff, both sea-going and shore-based, but also of her loyal "supporters' club". Members of the P.S.P.S. Scottish Branch have been tireless in their efforts to keep *Waverley* sailing and all sorts of individuals have made unique contributions to that on-going campaign.

Waverley is now the sole survivor of the fleets of steamships which since Henry Bell's *Comet* was launched in 1812 have criss-crossed the Firth of Clyde, carrying passengers and goods to remote communities and island villages, and also bringing pleasure to countless numbers of holiday makers who have enjoyed the beauties of the Firth of Clyde from their decks. Many people have happy memories of the Clyde Steamers: some are fortunate enough to be able to remember them in their pre-war heyday, but those whose memories stretch back only to the fifties and sixties will find in this book photographs which will remind them of the boats they once knew.

Some of the photographs in this book were taken by Montague Smith, a railway enthusiast and musician whose summer holidays each year gave him the opportunity to photograph Clyde steamers. Most, however, come from the collection of Ian Shannon, whose enthusiasm for *Waverley* took him the length and breadth of the United Kingdom each year as he followed the paddler to unusual ports of call. Following Ian Shannon's death in 1992, his collection of steamer photographs passed into the care of the P.S.P.S. Scottish Branch which was charged with the task of using them to help secure *Waverley*'s future. This book, drawing extensively on the Ian Shannon Collection, has been published to raise ever-needed funds for *Waverley* but also, we hope, to rekindle happy memories for those who shared Ian Shannon's love of the Firth of Clyde and its steamers.

A GREAT TRADITION

The tradition of steamers on the Clyde dates back to the appearance in 1812 of the tiny *Comet* – the first commercial steamship in Europe. The trade developed quickly as people began to have leisure time when they could escape, even if only for a day at a time, from the industrial centres. From very early days, the hub of steamer services was the island resort of Rothesay, and there was no better place to observe the continual coming and going of steamers.

(Left)
This view of a packed Rothesay pier shows *Columba* (nearest the camera), *Lord of the Isles* and one of the Caledonian Steam Packet Co. ferry class paddlers.

(Below)
Queen's Birthday Holiday, 1899. The C.S.P.'s *Marchioness of Lorne* and *Duchess of Rothesay* are double berthed, and again the pier is very crowded. The photograph was taken from *Davaar*, which was on a special day excursion from Campbeltown.

(Opposite top)
Queen-Empress loading passengers at Rothesay, with *Duchess of Rothesay* in Berth 3. The *Duchess*'s black, red and yellow funnel indicates the date to be 1923 or 1924.

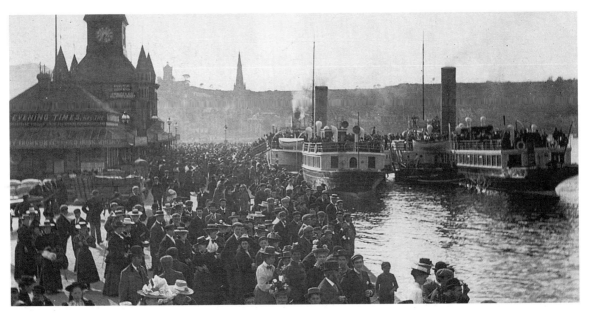

(*Below*) A 1929 view, with *Kylemore* alongside and *Jupiter* manœuvring. *Jupiter* was originally a Glasgow and South Western Railway steamer, and carried their attractive livery of grey hulls with black and red funnels.

After the Caledonian and G.& S.W. Railways were absorbed into the L.M.S. in 1923 the uniform eventually adopted was black hulls with black and buff funnels, as shown here.

THE "GLASGOW BOATS"

(*Left*)
A well-filled *Kylemore* arriving at Dunoon on Glasgow Fair Monday 1929, probably on a relief sailing from Glasgow to Rothesay. During the 1939-45 war she became a net-layer, and was sunk in 1940.

(*Below*)
Queen-Empress served in both wars, getting as far as the White Sea in the north of Russia in the first, and minesweeping off the south of England in the second. In 1946 she was found to be not worth reconditioning, and scrapped.

(*Right*)

A deck view on board *Queen-Empress*. This useful little steamer was to be found in all parts of the Firth, including Inveraray, Campbeltown, Girvan and Glasgow. When she became a railway steamer in the 1930s she also took a share of ferry duties.

(*Middle*)

Eagle III moored at the buoy in Rothesay Bay. Until the 1939-45 war, the three-berth pier at Rothesay was often so busy that a steamer which was scheduled to remain in Rothesay for some time had to clear the pier and tie up to a buoy like this.

(*Bottom*)

In the 1939-45 war, *Eagle III* was commissioned under the name H.M.S. *Oriole*. She took part in the evacuation from Dunkirk, where she was beached for 12 hours – an event shown in this dramatic photograph. *Eagle III* was also scrapped on her return from war service.

THE L.N.E.R. FLEET PRE-WAR

(*Right*) *Kenilworth* was built in 1898 for the North British Steam Packet Company, forerunner of the London & North Eastern Railway. She spent her life on fairly mundane sailings from the L.N.E.R. base at Craigendoran to Rothesay, and was broken up in 1938, a few years after her sister ship, the first *Talisman*.

(*Below*) This fine steamer, bearing the famous name *Waverley*, was built in 1899 to encourage excursion traffic from Craigendoran. After almost 40 years of stalwart service, interrupted only by minesweeping in the Great War, she was withdrawn from service at the end of the 1938 season, and would have been scrapped but for the intervention of another war. She again became a minesweeper, but met her end off Dunkirk in 1940. Her wreck was discovered by a diver in 1986.

(*Above*) *Marmion*, too, spent much of her life cruising from Craigendoran, although she also took her share of ferry duties. She survived three trips to Dunkirk, but was sunk by air attack at Harwich the following year. She is here seen off Dunoon, while the L.M.S. paddler *Mercury* passes beyond.

(*Below*) The first 52 years of *Lucy Ashton*'s service were unspectacular, but when her sisters were requisitioned for war service in 1939 she was left to carry on the Craigendoran services alone. This she did faithfully for the next six years, and survived to become a member of the post-war fleet based at Craigendoran.

THE L.M.S. FLEET PRE-WAR

Some members of the Gourock-based fleet were owned by the London, Midland & Scottish Railway, while others were retained in the ownership of the Caledonian Steam Packet, as this gave wider running powers. Effectively, however, they were all controlled by the L.M.S.

(*Above*) *Glen Rosa* was the last survivor of the fleet of the G.& S.W.R., which had amalgamated with the Caledonian Railway in 1923 to form part of the L.M.S., in whose colours the steamer is seen here. She was of an unusual design, with her low foredeck, and was strongly built so that she could undertake the Arran run in winter. She just avoided a second spell of war service by being withdrawn at the end of the 1938 season and scrapped shortly afterwards.

(*Below*) The *Mercury* of 1934 was a near-sister of *Caledonia*, but the former was built by Fairfield and the latter by Denny. *Mercury*'s career was spent on general ferry duties, rarely venturing further than the Kyles of Bute. Requisitioned as a minesweeper, she was damaged by striking a mine on Christmas Day 1940, and sank after a valiant attempt by *Caledonia* to tow her to port.

(*Above*) The last steamers built before the war were the sisters *Jupiter* and *Juno* in 1937. *Juno* is shown here leaving Rothesay during her very short Clyde career. Requisitioned for war service, she eventually became an anti-aircraft ship on the Thames, and was destroyed when a bomb fell between the funnels during an air raid in March 1941.

(*Right*) *Duchess of Rothesay* was built for the C.S.P. in 1895, and served until the outbreak of war in 1939, being particularly associated for many years with the Arran via Kyles cruise, and later with ferry runs and Kyles sailings. She was not reconditioned after the war, but was scrapped in 1946.

P.S. LUCY ASHTON

(Above)

The venerable *Lucy* is seen here in early wartime condition, still retaining her L.N.E.R. funnel colouring and before the fitting of a bombproof wheelhouse. *Lucy* carried on all the Craigendoran services alone throughout the war, except for ten days in the spring of 1944 following damage to a paddle wheel.

(Below)

Lucy Ashton at her home port, Craigendoran, with the diesel-electric *Talisman* in the next berth. The restoration of the attractive L.N.E.R. colours in 1946 was unfortunately short-lived, as nationalisation in 1948 resulted in the disappearance of the black, white and red funnel from the Clyde scene for 25 years.

(Above)
Lucy was not to bear the black and buff funnel of the British Railways fleet for long. She was finally withdrawn from passenger service in February 1949 and sold for breaking up at Faslane on the Gare Loch.

(Right)
The main engine is removed from the ship and is about to join the boiler on the quayside. Surprisingly, a reprieve was still to come. The hull was purchased by the British Shipbuilding Research Association for experiments in hull resistance. At Dumbarton, she was fitted with jet engines – to avoid disturbing the water – and she spent some time running noisily in the Gare Loch. Her scrapping was finally completed in 1951.

T.S. KING EDWARD

King Edward was one of the most significant ships in maritime history – when built by Denny in 1901 she was the world's first passenger turbine steamer. Her original owners, the Turbine Steamer Syndicate, placed her on their excursions from Greenock to Campbeltown or Inveraray. In 1927 she began her long association with the sailings from Glasgow, on which she spent the rest of her peacetime career. During the 1914-18 war she was used as a cross-Channel troopship, and later became an ambulance transport in the White Sea in the north of Russia. She had a less exciting time in the 1939-45 war, which she spent on tendering duties based at Gourock.

(*Right*)
Two veteran turbine steamers approaching the end of their sailing careers. *Duchess of Argyll* (left) and *King Edward* meet off Keppel Pier in 1951. Although the *Edward* was scrapped at Troon the following year, the *Duchess* was sold to the Admiralty for conversion to a floating laboratory, and she served in this capacity in Portland Harbour until 1970, when she was finally sold for breaking up.

(*Below*)
Live entertainment was a very long-standing tradition on Clyde Steamers. This typical trio played on *King Edward* in 1951.

T.S. DUCHESS OF ARGYLL

(*Above*) When *Duchess of Argyll* was built for the Caledonian Steam Packet Co. in 1906 she had the open foredeck at main deck level which was typical of their fleet. She is shown here arriving at Whiting Bay in that condition, although the large saloon windows are boarded up for the winter.

(*Below*) The main changes to *Duchess of Argyll*'s appearance over the years were the plating up of the bow in 1910 (to allow her to be used on the Stranraer - Larne run on occasion) and the adoption of black tops on her funnels in 1923. This 1931 photograph shows how well she looked in this condition.

(*Above*) Although *Duchess of Argyll* saw service in the Great War in the English Channel, she remained on the Clyde during the 1939-45 war, tendering to troopships and relieving on ferry services. In this view she is seen performing the latter duty.

(*Below*) A crosstrees was fitted to the mast during the war, and she acquired a wooden wheelhouse in 1948, as shown in this 1951 photograph of her nearing Rothesay.

P.S. DUCHESS OF FIFE

(*Above*) One of the most popular steamers of her time, with an active life of half a century, *Duchess of Fife* was supplied by Fairfield's in 1903 for general ferry work. She is seen leaving Rothesay in 1936.

(*Below*) She was employed as a minesweeper in both wars, and included four trips to Dunkirk in May 1940. On her return to the Clyde she was given a very thorough reconditioning by Lamont's of Port Glasgow.

(*Above*) *Duchess of Fife* was in commission all the year round, and is shown here boarded up for winter services. The wooden wheelhouse dates from 1948 – a long overdue concession to the climate in the west of Scotland.

(*Below*) The final alteration to *Duchess of Fife's* appearance was the fitting of wooden dodgers on the bridge to replace the earlier canvas, and it is in this condition that she is seen in this shot of her leaving Rothesay in her penultimate season, 1952.

T.S. GLEN SANNOX

(*Above*) As her name suggests, *Glen Sannox* was built specifically for the Arran service, where she spent almost all her working life, apart from a wartime stint assisting with troop movements between Larne and Stranraer. She did, however, cruise from the upper Firth occasionally, especially on Sundays, as is shown by this view of her arriving at Dunoon. When launched at Dumbarton in 1925 she was rather an anachronism, being modelled on the 19-year-old *Duchess of Argyll*, and this may have partly accounted for her relatively short career.

(*Below*) She continued to serve Arran during the war, and is seen here leaving Brodick around 5.30 on a summer's morning in 1944. When peace returned she remained the principal Arran steamer until her withdrawal in 1953.

(*Right*) To date there have been three ships bearing the name *Glen Sannox,* the turbine being the second of these. The first was a notable paddle steamer built at Clydebank in 1892 for the G.& S.W.R. Like her successor, she rarely deviated from the Arran run, and is seen here in Lamlash Bay. Her last season in service was 1924, after which she was scrapped at Port Glasgow.

(*Below*) The third *Glen Sannox* was a car ferry built at Troon, again for the Arran service, in 1957, and this was her almost exclusive employment until early 1970. Thereafter she had a very varied career, seeing service on various Clyde ferry routes, becoming the main Clyde cruising "steamer" for her owners, and, following the integration of the C.S.P. and MacBrayne organisations, sailing extensively among the Western Isles. She is seen here making a very rare visit to Tarbert, Loch Fyne, on a special excursion. She was withdrawn from service in June 1989 and two months later left for a new career in the Red Sea, bearing the name *Knooz*.

P.S. MARCHIONESS OF LORNE

(Above)
This neat little paddler was provided by Fairfield's in 1935 for the Gourock to Holy Loch service. She was quite similar to the same yard's *Mercury* of the previous year, but much smaller and with no passenger access to the upper deck.

(Below)
Marchioness of Lorne was the only "south bank" paddler not to be requisitioned for war service, and she continued on the Holy Loch run. Her task became more difficult as the Tail of the Bank and the Upper Firth assumed ever greater importance as an anchorage.

(Above)

Despite her size, *Marchioness of Lorne* had a triple expansion engine, but even this did not allow her service speed to exceed twelve knots. On the appearance of the first of the *Maid* class vessels she was transferred to the Millport service, but one season was enough to prove that her speed was inadequate and she was sold for scrap after only 19 years' service.

(Right)

On the Holy Loch service, with its frequent pier calls, the *Lorne*'s speed was no great disadvantage, and she was popular not only with the residents of the area but with afternoon cruise passengers from Gourock. She is seen here in 1951 approaching Hunter's Quay.

23

T.S. MARCHIONESS OF GRAHAM

(*Above*)
In 1936, the Fairfield yard built *Marchioness of Graham*, a twin-screw turbine steamer of a size and design similar to the paddle steamers *Mercury* and *Caledonia*.

(*Below*)
Although intended primarily for the Ardrossan - Arran service, she was also used for cruising, and is seen here in Rothesay Bay in 1938.

A well filled *Marchioness* leaving Ardrossan for Whiting Bay in 1957.

Marchioness of Graham was made redundant on the appearance of M.V. *Glen Sannox* in 1957, although she remained in service as spare steamer for the rest of that summer, and was later sold to the Diapoulis Line for further service in Greek waters. This photograph shows her in Queen's Dock, Glasgow, in February 1959, a few days prior to her departure for Piraeus, the port of Athens. Her decks are filled with sacks of coal – sufficient to take her to Gibraltar, where she refuelled.

It is difficult to believe that the motor vessel *Ellas*, pictured here at Piraeus, is the former steamer *Marchioness of Graham*, but a comparison of small details such as the positioning of portholes will confirm that it is. At first she was used on the service to Rhodes, but later, under a succession of owners and several different names, she was engaged in cruising. She was finally scrapped in 1975.

P.S. JUPITER

Jupiter was, by about six weeks, the elder of the 1937 twins from the Fairfield yard at Govan. She was designed for both summer and winter service on the basic Dunoon and Rothesay ferry runs. After war service as H.M.S. *Scawfell* consisting of a spell as a minesweeper and later conversion to an anti-aircraft ship, she returned to Clyde service in 1946. Towards the end of her life she was associated with a Sunday afternoon cruise from Glasgow to Lochgoilhead, and also with the Cumbrae Circle cruise. 1957 was her last season, but she remained in Greenock's Albert Harbour until 1961, when she was sold to Dublin for breaking up.

(*Above*) The previous *Jupiter* was built at Clydebank for the G.&S.W.R. in 1896, and employed on the Arran via Kyles of Bute cruise until the outbreak of war in 1914. She was a minesweeper in the English Channel, and after reconversion for peacetime duties became associated with the Greenock - Ayr route. She was sold for scrap after the 1935 season.

(*Above*) The name *Jupiter* was perpetuated by being bestowed on this car ferry in 1974. Like her predecessor, she also has a slightly younger identical twin named *Juno*. Although intended for the Dunoon and Rothesay services, she was given additional equipment in 1983 which allowed her to undertake relief runs to Brodick, where she is shown in this photograph. In 1993 her horizons were broadened further by allocating her twice-weekly cruises to Tighnabruaich.

T.S. SAINT COLUMBA

This steamer had an interesting history, having been built by Denny in 1912 as *Queen Alexandra*. She was a consort for *King Edward*, and replaced an earlier *Queen Alexandra* which had been badly damaged by fire the previous year. Her early years were spent mainly on the Campbeltown sailings, although after serving in the Great War she sailed to Inveraray for some years. When she was bought by David MacBrayne Ltd in 1935 to replace their famous *Columba*,

she was altered, most noticeably by having her original two funnels replaced by three, and was renamed *Saint Columba*. During her career with MacBrayne's, she was used exclusively on their premier route – the "Royal Route" to Tarbert and Ardrishaig.

(*Opposite top*)
In 1950, when this photograph was taken, she had daily duels with *Duchess of Montrose* in the Kyles of Bute. The size of her bow wave indicates the extent to which she is trying to overtake her rival.

(*Opposite below*)
Arriving at Dunoon.

(*Above*)
The MacBrayne livery was very similar to that of the Cunard Line, as they had had a common origin (in very early days MacBrayne funnels included black hoops). This shot shows a meeting of the two, as *Saint Columba* encounters one of the Cunard quartette of the mid-50s, probably *Carinthia* or *Sylvania*.

(*Below*)
Saint Columba at Rothesay late in her career. She was withdrawn at the end of the 1958 season, and broken up at Port Glasgow the following year.

T.S. DUCHESS OF MONTROSE

(*Above*) This superb steamer was delivered by Denny in 1930 to the C.S.P. to win back some of the cruising market from rival companies, notably Turbine Steamers Ltd. Built as a "first-class only" ship, she was given a schedule of fast, long distance cruises from Gourock and proved an instant success. From 1952 she often relieved the Glasgow Bridge Wharf steamer on peak days, and also visited Glasgow for charters. She is seen here leaving Bridge Wharf in May 1954.

(*Below*) Approaching Rothesay pier on a summer's day in 1959.

(*Above*) With the exception of two months in 1940 assisting with troop movements at Stranraer, *Duchess of Montrose* remained on the Wemyss Bay - Rothesay service throughout the war. The schedule included a number of calls at Innellan, and occasional weekend sailings to Largs and Keppel. This photograph shows her in early wartime condition.

(*Right*) Later in the war she was fitted with a steel wheelhouse and had her name obliterated. A detachable board identifies her as "D OF M'ROSE".

(*Below*) By April 1946 some semblance of peacetime colours had been restored, although there was clearly a long way to go.

(*Above*) *Duchess of Montrose* soon settled down to a programme of long distance cruises from Gourock with destinations including Inveraray, Campbeltown and round Ailsa Craig. She continued in this employment until August 1964.

(*Below*) *Duchess of Montrose* arriving in the Albert Harbour on 31st August 1964 – her very last manœuvre under her own power. The fine condition of her paintwork at the end of a busy season is particularly noteworthy. A year later she was towed to Ghent and broken up.

P.S. JEANIE DEANS

(*Above*) The L.N.E.R.'s reply to the L.M.S. *Duchess of Montrose* was this fine paddler, *Jeanie Deans*. She was built by Fairfield's in 1931, and was the largest steamer ever to be based at Craigendoran. In her original condition she had no deck saloons and very short funnels, as shown here. She spent her first season on the Lochgoilhead and Arrochar service, with a Sunday cruise round Bute.

(*Below*) After one season, *Jeanie* was fitted with an observation saloon on the foredeck. Unusually, the funnels were lengthened by different amounts, giving a very distinctive profile. She was given a programme of cruises which more nearly rivalled the *Montrose*'s – for example, to Ayr, round Arran and round Ailsa Craig.

(*Above*) Following a wartime career as a minesweeper and anti-aircraft ship, *Jeanie Deans* was extensively reconditioned by A. & J. Inglis, being substantially altered in the process. She was given two new funnels of equal height, an after deck shelter and a mainmast. Resplendent in the restored L.N.E.R. livery, she added colour and character to the Clyde scene.

(*Below*) With the nationalisation of the railways in 1948, *Jeanie Deans*, the largest paddle steamer in the British Railways fleet, lost her red, white and black funnel colours. This view is of her approaching Gourock with her buff and black funnels and white deckhouses.

(*Above*) *Jeanie's* engine room was broadly similar to that of the present *Waverley*. Second Engineer James Sweeney is seen at the controls, accompanied by a fireman known as Barney.

(*Below*) After several years of being restricted to the undemanding cruise round Bute, with weekend sailings to Tighnabruaich, *Jeanie* was revitalised in 1961-64 by alternating rosters weekly with *Waverley*. This took her to piers at all corners of the Firth such as Arrochar and Brodick which she had not visited regularly since the 1930s. She was sold in 1965 for further service on the Thames under the name *Queen of the South*, but the venture was not a success and after two disastrous seasons she was sold for scrap, being towed to Antwerp in December 1967.

D.E.P.V. TALISMAN

(*Above*) Although looking like a conventional Clyde steamer, Diesel Electric Paddle Vessel *Talisman* had a propulsion system that was unique. Four diesel engines were coupled to generators, and a large electric motor was mounted on the paddle shaft. Other diesel-electric paddlers had their motors geared to the paddle shaft, or were connected by chains – it was the direct mounting of the motor on the shaft which was *Talisman*'s unique feature. This view shows the ship in her pre-war condition.

(*Below*) Renamed H.M.S. *Aristocrat* for a distinguished war career, *Talisman* returned to Clyde service in 1946. Comparison with the previous photograph shows that she had been altered during her reconditioning. She resumed her pre-war service on the Craigendoran - Rothesay - Kyles of Bute sailings.

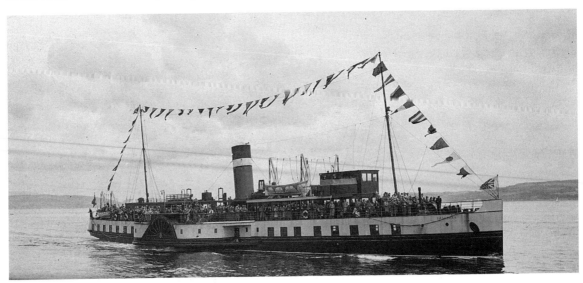

Like *Jeanie Deans* and *Lucy Ashton*, *Talisman* became a member of the British Railways fleet in 1948, whereupon her funnel became buff and black.

Talisman was withdrawn from the Craigendoran services in 1953 on the appearance of *Maid of Argyll*, and was threatened with the scrapyard. Her reprieve came about as a result of complaints about *Marchioness of Lorne*'s speed on the Millport run. *Talisman* was re-engined with new diesels and became the Millport "steamer", apart from appearances on her old station in spring most years. She was also for many years the standby vessel at Gourock for part of the winter.

This view (*middle*) shows her leaving Fairlie in 1956. Her paddleboxes became white that year due to the influence of an ex-L.M.S. captain, who defiled *Waverley*'s paddleboxes in the same way three years later.

Talisman was finally withdrawn from service late in 1966 and was scrapped at Dalmuir the following year.

THE ARDRISHAIG MAIL

The most prestigious route on the Clyde was probably that of MacBrayne's mail steamer to Ardrishaig, the first stage in the "Royal Route" to the Highlands. Until 1939 the departure was from Glasgow (at 7.00 a.m. originally, later 7.11 a.m.), although during both wars the service started at Wemyss Bay. From 1946 the sailing was from Gourock, until it finally disappeared from the Clyde scene in 1969.

One of the most famous ships ever to sail on the route was the paddle steamer *Iona*. She came from the Clydebank yard of J. & G. Thomson in 1864, and served as the Ardrishaig mail steamer in the peak summer months until the arrival of *Columba* in 1878. Thereafter she often sailed to Ardrishaig in early and late season and performed the famous Sacred Isle cruise to Iona and Staffa in mid-summer. She was withdrawn in 1935 and broken up, alongside *Columba*, at Dalmuir.

(*Below*) T.S. *King George V*, seen here arriving at Tarbert, began life in 1926 as a Clyde steamer, sailing on the Turbine Steamers Ltd services to Inveraray and Campbeltown. She was sold to David MacBrayne Ltd in 1935, and began a long association with the cruise from Oban to Staffa and Iona, which lasted until her withdrawal in 1974. She did return to the Clyde on rare occasions and sailed on the Loch Fyne route, notably throughout the summer of 1946 when *Saint Columba* was not available.

(*Above*) *Lochfyne*, the first diesel electric vessel built for service in Britain, entered the MacBrayne fleet in 1931. Before the war she cruised from Oban in summer and took over the Ardrishaig run in winter. She spent most of the war years on the latter service, and returned to the earlier arrangement from 1947 till 1958. Following the demise of *Saint Columba*, she became the mail "steamer" all the year round, except when relieved by *Lochnevis* for overhaul or for a short spring season from Oban. She was withdrawn in 1969.

(*Below*) In many respects a smaller version of *Lochfyne*, the diesel-electric *Lochnevis* of 1934 relieved on the mail run on a regular basis although from 1950 the winter service terminated at Tarbert. *Lochnevis* was also withdrawn in 1969, and was sold to Dutch owners.

P.S. CALEDONIA

(*Above*) The first steamer to be built for the Caledonian Steam Packet Co. was named *Caledonia*. She was originally associated with services to Rothesay, but for many years was well known as the Holy Loch steamer. She was withdrawn in 1933.

(*Below*) The second *Caledonia*, a Denny product of 1934, was intended for all year round service to Dunoon and Rothesay, with short cruises in summer. She was strongly built to withstand the rigours of the winter service to Arran if required, qualities which served her well during war service as H.M.S. *Goatfell*. This photograph shows her arriving at Dunoon in her first season.

(*Opposite top*)

Caledonia, with her Class V passenger complement of 1730, was often employed on up-Firth ferry duties in the early and late seasons. From 1954 till 1964 she was the Ayr excursion steamer in mid-summer, on a schedule which included Ardrossan - Arran services at weekends and on other days of peak traffic. In the early and late seasons, she had a wide variety of duties, often standing in for other steamers when necessary.

(*Opposite below*)

From 1965 until her withdrawal in 1969, she was based at Craigendoran in succession to *Jeanie Deans*, and it is during this phase of her life that she is seen here arriving at Gourock.

(*Above*) *Caledonia*'s triple expansion engine was of a distinctive design, quite different from the other Clyde steamers. It was fitted with Brock valve gear, a patent of her builders. The engine survives, in working condition, in a museum at Liphook in Hampshire.

(*Below*) This view shows how well-concealed the paddleboxes could appear from some angles. These were a feature of all the L.M.S. paddlers of the 1930s. *Caledonia* was sold to Bass Charrington Ltd in 1971 and towed to the Thames, where she became a restaurant moored beside Waterloo Bridge. One night in April 1980 she caught fire and was damaged beyond repair, although her engine was salvaged.

T.S. DUCHESS OF HAMILTON

(*Above*) *Duchess of Hamilton* was virtually a repeat of *Duchess of Montrose*, but was built in 1932 by Harland & Wolff, Govan, the machinery coming from that company's Belfast works. From 1932 till 1939 she was the Ayr excursion steamer. She spent the war years on the Clyde as a tender, except for two periods as a troopship at Stranraer. On her return to peacetime work she was put on a programme of day cruises from Gourock, complementing that of *Duchess of Montrose*. She is seen here arriving at Rothesay in 1951...

(*Below*)

...and at Brodick a few years later. There were several slight differences between the two sisters. The *Hamilton* had a crosstrees on the mainmast, and the grouping of windows on the main deck was different. The funnels were also of different proportions and at a different rake from the *Montrose*'s.

(Above)
Duchess of Hamilton is shown here coming into Dunoon in August 1965 in the new colour scheme, which included "Monastral" blue hull and lions rampant on the funnels.

(Left)
The *Hamilton* shows her power of acceleration as she pulls away from the pier.

(Opposite top)
With a considerable list to starboard, *Duchess of Hamilton* cruises slowly past John Brown's Clydebank shipyard, where *Queen Elizabeth 2* is almost ready for launching.

(Opposite below)
The corresponding scene some 33 years earlier, as *Queen-Empress* passes the ship that was soon to become *Queen Mary*.

T.S. QUEEN MARY/QUEEN MARY II

(*Opposite top*)

The best fitted-out steamer ever to be built for the White Funnel sailings from Glasgow was the turbine *Queen Mary,* which came from Denny's in 1933. As is well known, she was renamed *Queen Mary II* in 1935 to allow her original name to be used on the Cunarder.

(*Opposite below*)

Before the war, and for the first few seasons after it, her normal employment was the 10 a.m. cruise to the Arran coast, although she also visited the Kyles of Bute. This is the scene in this post-war photograph, taken from *Caledonia.*

(*Above*) After serving on the Dunoon ferry runs during the war, and tendering at the Tail of the Bank, the *Mary* returned to the Glasgow cruises in 1946 as consort to *King Edward.* To comply with new lighting regulations, she was fitted with a mainmast in 1953, and is shown here in this condition in Glasgow, with *Maid of Cumbrae* sailing past.

(*Below*) In 1957, *Queen Mary II* was re-boilered, and had her two funnels replaced by a single large one.

(*Above*) By 1968, when this photograph was taken, *Queen Mary II* had acquired lions on her funnel and a blue hull. Her appearance was not improved when, in the spring of 1969, her masts were shortened to allow her to sail under the Kingston Bridge, then nearing completion. The Bridge Wharf sailings were abandoned at the end of that season, and she transferred to cruising from Gourock.

(*Below*) When the C.S.P. amalgamated with David MacBrayne Ltd in 1973, the combined fleet adopted red funnels with black tops, and with the Caledonian lion in

a yellow circle. *Queen Mary* (the *"II"* was dropped in 1976 when the Cunarder was sold to the U.S.A.) is seen here leaving Rothesay in this livery, while the car ferries *Arran* and *Cowal* lie at the pier. Following her withdrawal in 1977 there were several schemes to moor her in Glasgow as a restaurant or a museum, but these did not come to fruition. She was sold to new owners who had her towed to the Thames, restored her to something approximating to her original appearance and moored her as a restaurant in the berth previously occupied by *Caledonia*.

LOCH LOMOND STEAMERS

From the earliest days of steam navigation, services on Loch Lomond were effectively an extension of the Clyde network, and many of the steamers were owned by companies which were also Clyde steamer operators.

(*Above*) The Loch steamers were slightly smaller versions of the typical Clyde steamers of the same era. *Princess May*, here shown at Tarbet, was launched at A.&J. Inglis' Pointhouse shipyard in October 1898, and sailed up the River Leven to the Loch the following month. Her sister ship, *Prince George*, dating from the same year, was broken up in 1942.

(*Below*) This interesting photograph, taken in January 1953, shows *Maid of the Loch* nearing completion on the slipway. *Prince Edward* is alongside the pier while *Princess May* lies at anchor in the bay awaiting her fate. Notice that the *Maid*'s funnel has a deep black top; this was painted over shortly before her launch to give an all-buff funnel. It is also of interest that there is a railway track leading to the side of the slipway – two wagons can be seen on the right.

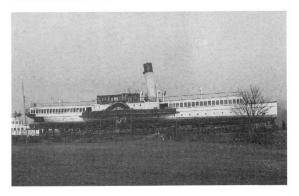

(*Above*)

Maid of the Loch, another Inglis product, was given British Railways Inland Waterways livery – white hull, green underbody and buff funnel – and *Prince Edward*, for her last two seasons, was painted in the same colour scheme. This photograph shows the transformation almost complete. The funnel has retained its black top, and although a plain buff funnel was tried for a time, it quickly became stained with soot, and the black top was restored. When *Maid of the Loch* appeared in 1953, *Princess May* was scrapped at Balloch, but *Prince Edward* continued to sail for a further two years.

(*Opposite*)

Inversnaid is the setting for this attractive view of passengers coming ashore from *Maid of the Loch*. She was sold early in 1982 to a brewery, which neither operated the ship nor took any steps to preserve her, although they did have ambitious plans for her future use. They acquired the former C.S.P. motor boat *Countess of Breadalbane*, transported her to Balloch, renamed her *Countess Fiona* and ran a programme of cruises with her. From 1989 the two ships passed through the hands of successive owners but the *Maid* continued to be neglected. In December 1992 they were acquired by Dumbarton District Council, with an input from the Paddle Steamer Preservation Society who soon took steps to try to arrest the deterioration.

(*Below*)

The largest vessel ever to sail on an inland waterway in Britain, *Maid of the Loch* brought new standards of comfort and on-board facilities to the Loch. However, post-war passenger numbers never reached their expected level, and the *Maid* was under constant threat of withdrawal from 1961 onwards. She is shown here at Ardlui, the most northerly of her calling points. Notice the British Railways insignia on her bows.

(*Below*) To emphasise the change of ownership, and to indicate to the public that an interest was being taken in the ship, this eye-catching colour scheme was adopted during the summer of 1993. The *Maid'*s graceful lines, previously obscured by the all-white colour scheme, were now revealed for the first time.

MEMORIES . . . .

(*Above*) *Queen Mary II* at Keppel pier, with M.V. *Keppel* and the C.S.P.'s HM2-011 hovercraft passing. The hovercraft, nicknamed the "scooshin' cushion", was a short-lived venture in 1970-71 which had limited success.

(*Below*) It is tempting to caption this photograph "Paw, Maw and the Weans". *Queen Mary II, Duchess of Hamilton, Maid of Cumbrae* and *Countess of Breadalbane* in Greenock's East India Harbour – for many years the winter lay-up berth of the C.S.P. fleet

The Caledonian Steam Packet Co. was renowned for the ornate decoration on the paddle boxes of its steamers. Here is the port side of *Duchess of Fife*.

The paddle boxes of the L.N.E.R.'s *Jeanie Deans* bore portraits of Sir Walter Scott's heroine.

The British Transport Commission chose a design based on Celtic knotwork to enhance the paddle boxes of *Maid of the Loch*.

When *Davaar* was built at Govan in
1885 for the Campbeltown & Glasgow
Steam Packet Co. Ltd she had two
funnels, but in 1903 she was re-
boiled and returned to service with
one funnel. Apart from occasional
special excursions, she spent her entire
life on the Glasgow - Campbeltown
route. This was discontinued in 1940,
and *Davaar* was scrapped in 1943.
She is seen here at the Broomielaw,
with the Clyde Navigation Trust
building in the background.

In 1948 a company was formed to
provide a service from Glasgow to
Campbeltown using the motor vessel
Wimaisia, this unusual name being
formed from the first two letters of
the names of the owner, his wife, his
daughter and his son. She had been
built in Belfast in 1936 as the tug/
tender *Duchess of Abercorn*, and this
photograph shows her first arrival in
Campbeltown, on 1st June 1948. The
venture was not a success, and
Wimaisia was sold to Liverpool Fire
Service for further operation.

Minard was built in Bowling in 1926
for Clyde Cargo Steamers Ltd. and
served most ports on the Firth, mainly
those in Loch Fyne. She became
redundant shortly after car ferry
services were introduced on the Clyde
in the mid-1950s.

(*Above*) A familiar sight in Rothesay from 1938 until her sale in 1988 was the small motor vessel *Gay Queen*. She performed daily cruises to the Kyles of Bute and nearby lochs, and one of her advertised attractions on these was "the Voice of the Skipper". Her new owners operate her from Poole, Dorset, under the name *Alice-Marie*.

(*Below*) A motor vessel of similar size, also based at Rothesay and offering similar cruises, was *Maid of Bute*. In 1965-66 she was chartered weekly in mid-summer by the C.S.P. to provide a Friday evening connection from Rothesay to Tighnabruaich, returning on the Saturday morning. She was sold in 1973 for further cruising from Fort William, and some years later appeared as *Maid of the Forth* on the Firth of Forth, being subsequently sold for service at Southend.

THE MOTOR SHIP ERA

(*Right*)

This motor vessel has had, perhaps, the most varied career of all. She was built in 1936 by Denny, taken in sections by rail to Loch Awe, re-assembled at the lochside and named *Countess of Breadalbane*. In 1952 she was taken by road to Inveraray and then towed to Dumbarton where she was altered by her builders to fit her for the Largs - Millport service and short cruises. In 1971 she was acquired by W. R. Ritchie of Gourock who used her on his Helensburgh and Kilmun services, for which she was renamed *Countess of Kempock*. She was bought in 1978 by Offshore Workboats Ltd, who based her at Ulva Ferry on Mull for cruises to Staffa and Iona. Four years

later she was sold to Ind Coope, owners of *Maid of the Loch*, and taken on her second road journey – from Stobcross Quay, Glasgow, to Balloch. Renamed *Countess Fiona*, and with a (dummy) funnel and two masts, she began a new career cruising on Loch Lomond. In the 1988-89 winter she was substantially altered, being given a full-width saloon, a new funnel and new masts. Since the following winter she has remained on the slipway at Balloch, and was sold along with *Maid of the Loch* to Dumbarton District Council in December 1992. Her future is now uncertain.

(*Left*)

The motor ship era began in earnest for the C.S.P. on 17th February 1953 when *Maid of Ashton* was launched at Yarrow's Scotstoun yard. The four *Maids* (*of Ashton, Argyll, Skelmorlie* and *Cumbrae*) were originally intended to have a single, fairly short mast, and, as shown here, *Maid of Ashton* was actually launched in this condition. New lighting regulations made a mainmast necessary, and the foremast was also lengthened. She spent each summer until 1966 based on the Holy Loch run, and thereafter, until her withdrawal in 1971, she rotated duties with the other three *Maids*. She was sold in January 1973 to the Yardarm Club in London, and was moored beside Hungerford Bridge with the name *Hispaniola*. She remains there to this day, and despite having had her superstructure extended she is still quite recognisable.

(*Above*)

A further quantum leap forward for the C.S.P. came later in 1953 with the launch on 22nd September of M.V. *Arran* – the Clyde's first large car ferry. She entered service on 4th January 1954 (taking over the Dunoon roster from *Waverley*) and later shared duties with her sisters *Cowal* and *Bute* on the Dunoon, Rothesay, Millport and Brodick services. *Arran* was the first C.S.P. ship to sail regularly in the Western Isles when in 1970 she was chartered by David MacBrayne Ltd for the Islay service. She subsequently sailed on several West Highland routes, latterly converted to stern loading, and also appeared on Clyde services. In 1980 she was sold to Dublin to become a floating nightclub, and later was towed up the Manchester Ship Canal to Salford Docks for a similar role, renamed *Revolution*. She was finally broken up in 1992.

(*Right*)

Two of the 1953/54 motorships, the passenger-only *Maid of Cumbrae* and the car ferry *Cowal,* early in their careers. *Cowal* still has the "goal posts" aft which were replaced in 1959 by a tripod mast when the cargo hold was plated over. Both ships went east when their Clyde sailing days were over – in 1978 *Maid of Cumbrae*, which had been converted to a stern-loading car ferry in 1972, was sold for further service in the Bay of Naples renamed *Noce di Cocco* where she is a rival to *Ala* – formerly *Maid of Skelmorlie*! Though *Cowal* left for Piraeus the following spring, she was never actually put into service but later scrapped, a fate shared by *Bute*.

(*Above*) *Glen Sannox* was a later addition to the Clyde car ferry programme, and was in many respects an enlarged and improved version of *Arran, Bute* and *Cowal*. This atmospheric shot shows her at Gourock Pier.

(*Below*) In 1976, Caledonian MacBrayne resumed sailings from Glasgow, using the Waverley Terminal at Anderston Quay. *Glen Sannox* used this berth when relieving *Queen Mary* or when on charter. The shed immediately beyond the ship has since been demolished and the area landscaped.

(*Above*) *Keppel*, formerly the Tilbury ferry *Rose*, was built at Southampton in 1961 and bought by the C.S.P. in 1967 partly to replace *Talisman* at Millport, where she is seen with the Clyde Marine Motoring Co.'s *Rover*, built at Renfrew in 1964. *Maid of Argyll* is in the distance. After five years of providing cruises, *Keppel* was withdrawn at the end of 1992 and was sold to Greenock owners the following year for further cruising under the name *Clyde Rose*. *Maid of Argyll* was sold in 1972 to Greece where, named *City of Piraeus*, she cruises from Piraeus to the nearby islands as a consort of *City of Hydra*, the former MacBrayne *Claymore* of 1955. *Rover* remains in the Clyde Marine Motoring fleet.

(*Below*) 1970 saw another major advance for the C.S.P. when they introduced their first drive-through ferry. *Caledonia*, the third ship of that name in the company, had been built in Sweden in 1966 for the Stena Line. At first used in the Baltic and later on a Tilbury - Calais service, she arrived in the Clyde in January 1970 and underwent various alterations to conform to Department of Transport requirements. She served on the Arran run, summer and winter, until 1974 when she was transferred to the Oban - Craignure service in summer, but still returned to Arran in winter. She was sold out of the fleet in 1988, eventually going to the Red Sea pilgrim traffic. The other ferry is *Cowal*.

P.S. WAVERLEY

(*Above*) To compensate for the wartime loss of *Waverley* and *Marmion*, the L.N.E.R. ordered a new paddle steamer *Waverley* and had plans for a new *Marmion*. A.&J. Inglis launched *Waverley* in 1946, and she entered service the following summer on the route for which she had been intended – Craigendoran to Lochgoilhead and Arrochar. Nationalisation the following January resulted in the plans being abandoned for *Marmion*, which was to have become the main cruising steamer. In this photograph, *Waverley* is seen in the L.N.E.R. colours which she wore for only one season, arriving at Arrochar.

(*Below*) When she became a member of the British Railways fleet she lost her distinctive funnel colours, and in 1953 the deck saloons were painted white rather than stained to imitate wood. By this time the Arrochar cruise was on offer less frequently, and *Waverley* broadened her horizons to include cruises Round the Lochs and to Arran via the Kyles of Bute.

(*Above*) Minor changes to her appearance took place from time to time; for example, the paddleboxes became white in 1959. The forward funnel was replaced in 1961 by an all-welded one which no longer carried the extra stay-ring resulting from the L.N.E.R. colour scheme.

The after funnel was similarly replaced the following year, so this view of her arriving at Dunoon can definitely be dated as 1961.

(*Below*) Another 1961 shot shows her arriving at Gourock.

(*Above*) A further reorganisation in 1965 brought "Monastral" blue hulls and red lions on the funnels. In 1969 *Waverley*'s masts were shortened to allow her to pass under the Kingston Bridge in Glasgow, and the following year the hull reverted to black.

(*Below*) In July 1971 *Waverley* was blown heavily against Arrochar Pier, as a result of which she lost the top half of her foremast. She sailed with this unusual profile for the rest of the season, and is seen here in September leaving Wemyss Bay with *Glen Sannox* at the pier. A new foremast was fitted during the winter overhaul.

(*Above*) By 1972 it was clear that *Waverley* was the last paddle steamer in the world to have a certificate to carry passengers "deep sea" (beyond Cumbrae Heads in the case of the Clyde estuary). The Paddle Steamer Preservation Society persuaded her owners to highlight her uniqueness by painting the paddleboxes black. The P.S.P.S. chartered her in September for a cruise to Inveraray, and she is shown here arriving at the Loch Fyne port on that occasion.

(*Below*) On 1st January 1973 the C.S.P. and David MacBrayne Ltd combined to form Caledonian MacBrayne Ltd. Funnel colours reflected this merger, being red with black tops, and with Caledonian lions on yellow discs. *Waverley* is seen leaving Dunoon in that year, with *Countess of Kempock* in a very unusual berth.

(*Right*) The subsequent history of the ship is well known. Withdrawn by CalMac at the end of the 1973 season, she was presented to the P.S.P.S. the following year for the nominal sum of £1. She re-entered service in 1975 for Waverley Steam Navigation Co. Ltd with her 1947 funnel colours restored, and brought a welcome touch of colour and interest to the Firth. In this 1975 photograph she is seen berthing at the notoriously difficult solid stone pier at Largs, the manœuvre being made more tricky by a strong onshore wind.

(*Below*) In the years since the change in her ownership, *Waverley*'s appearance has changed in a number of details, many of which can be identified by comparing this photograph with the preceding one. The two gold lines round the hull, applied in 1993, restored an embellishment which had been absent for 40 years. *Waverley* is now the very last of the long line of Clyde Steamers which began with *Comet* in 1812.